United States
Department of
Agriculture

**Forest
Service**

**North Central
Research Station**

**General Technical
Report NC-255**

Creating FGDC and NBII Metadata With Metavist 2005

I0410989

David J. Rugg

Disclaimer

The computer program described in this publication is available on request with the understanding that the U.S. Department of Agriculture cannot assure its accuracy, completeness, reliability, or suitability for any other purpose than that reported. The recipient may not assert any proprietary rights thereto nor represent it to anyone as other than a Government-produced computer program.

Mention of trade names does not constitute endorsement by the USDA Forest Service.

Table of Contents

Creating FGDC and NBII Metadata With Metavist 2005

INTRODUCTION

Metavist 2005, a software tool for the metadata archivist, is used to create metadata compliant with two of the Federal Geographic Data Committee (FGDC) metadata standards—"FGDC Content Standard for Digital Geospatial Metadata" (FGDC 1998) and "FGDC Biological Data Profile of the Content Standard for Digital Geospatial Metadata" (FGDC 1999). This manual does not define the elements present in the standards. Rather, its purpose is simply to help you successfully use the software. Because thorough knowledge of metadata and the FGDC metadata standards are not prerequisites, a brief overview of those topics is provided.

Metadata Background

Definition of metadata

Metadata are data that describe data. Metadata are used to answer such questions as what data were collected, how they were collected, why they were collected, how reliable they are, and what issues should be accounted for when working with them. Metadata also describe how data are stored, how to access the data, what tools are needed to work with the data, and related matters. The most common objectives of metadata collection are to (1) provide internal data documentation, (2) enhance current data sharing, and (3) enhance the future utility of data archives.

The FGDC spatial metadata standard

Since 1995, the Federal Government has been required to create metadata for geospatial data it produces, and make those data available to the public (Executive Order 12906). The common understanding of geospatial data is that it references specific places on the planet via a coordinate system suitable for use on a map or in geographic information system (GIS) software. The FGDC was created to address how to deal with this requirement; use of its standard is mandatory for the Federal Government. Further information about the standard and related activities can be found at the FGDC's Web site (www.fgdc.gov). Two benefits of the formal standard are consistency of (1) documentation elements and (2) terminology. The known structure lends itself to automated searching for candidate data sets based on their metadata. To facilitate this, the FGDC operates the National Spatial Data Clearinghouse. The clearinghouse provides a way to conduct searches against the metadata and find what spatial data sets the Government has created (although the data sets themselves are not housed in the clearinghouse). In addition to delineating metadata for general geospatial data, the current version of the standard (FGDC 1998) provides a mechanism for other organizations to add elements and collections of elements, called "profiles."

About The Author:

David J. Rugg is Research Data Archivist with the USDA Forest Service, North Central Research Station, 1992 Folwell Ave., St. Paul, MN 55108; Phone: (651) 649-5173; e-mail: drugg@fs.fed.us.

The FGDC Biological Data Profile

A significant portion of biological research either has no spatial component or has substantial aspects besides the purely spatial. The National Biological Information Infrastructure (NBII), part of the Biological Resources Division of the U.S. Geological Survey (USGS), is responsible for developing a metadata standard covering such research. To accomplish this task, NBII developed a Biological Data Profile (FGDC 1999) to enhance the FGDC Standard. The NBII profile has been approved for use by the FGDC. While the profile is specifically designed for biological data, it is defined broadly enough to be applicable to other scientific research. Thus, the profile can be used to describe spatial data, nonspatial numeric data, and nonspatial nonnumeric data— just about anything of scientific interest. Further information about this profile, NBII's metadata clearinghouse, and other activities can be found at NBII's Web site (www.nbii.gov).

Organization of the metadata standard

As defined by the FGDC, the standard's elements are organized into 10 sections. There are seven main sections:

- Identification (mandatory),
- Data Quality Information,
- Spatial Data Organization Information,
- Spatial Reference Information,
- Entity and Attribute Information,
- Distribution Information, and
- Metadata Reference Information (mandatory).

The five sections that are not mandatory are all "mandatory if applicable": if a section is relevant to your data set then you have to fill in that section. The other three sections defined by the standard—Citation Information, Time Period Information, and Contact Information—are supporting sections that are referenced by the main sections. Each section contains a number of elements. Some of these are "simple" elements—items for which you provide information. Other elements are "compound"—elements that organize a related set of simple elements. The elements may be mandatory, mandatory if applicable, or optional. Optional elements do not need to be filled in, even if they are applicable.

Official definitions for the elements are provided by the FGDC (FGDC 1998, FGDC 1999); this manual does not reproduce those definitions. Another useful document is the metadata workbook (FGDC 2000). The FGDC (1998) manual and workbook can be found at the FGDC Web site (www.fgdc.gov); the Biological Profile manual can be found at the NBII Web site (www.nbii.gov). These documents are also included in the Metavist 2005 package and are installed in the application directory (default location c:\program files\metavist). The metadata workbook includes two spatial data examples—one for a USGS digital line graph, and one for National Wetlands Inventory wetlands data. Two additional examples documenting actual data sets are installed in the application directory; one describes an oceanographic data set (Schweitzer_oceanography.xml), the other a volcano atlas shape file (volcano.shp.xml) (ESRI 2003). Finally, a color-coded graphical overview of the standard is reproduced in appendix A. Printing the graphics prior to creating metadata is strongly

recommended. They are very helpful for both understanding the standard and recalling how information is organized when creating metadata.

XML Background

Storing metadata as XML

There are many formats for digitally storing metadata—word processor, spreadsheet, database, ASCII text, etc. Unfortunately, many of these formats do not work well across multiple computer platforms or need to have their format updated over time as versions of the creating software become obsolete. While text suffers less from these problems, it tends to be difficult to search. A relatively new technology that addresses these issues is Extensible Markup Language, XML. XML is a tag-based language, like HTML for the Web, but the tags are user-defined. It is stored in a modern text format using Unicode characters. The Unicode representation makes XML portable across all computing platforms and durable over time. By defining the tag structure, XML files can be searched fairly easily. To make the metadata available as widely as possible, facilitate automated searches, and minimize the effort required to maintain a usable format over time, Metavist 2005 uses XML as its native file format. The encoding for Unicode in the software is UTF-8.

Although you can view an XML document in a program like Windows Notepad, to fully understand the document you need to understand the tag structure. Tag structures can be defined using a document type definition or a schema; Metavist uses the newer schema approach. The schema, contained in ncMetadata.xsd, is provided as part of the installation. Because the schema defines what a proper document looks like for this application, it can be used to verify that a particular XML document structure conforms to the metadata formatting requirements. This verification checks for required tags and for the proper formatting of element content—number, date, text, etc. However, comparing a candidate document to the schema cannot tell you whether mandatory if applicable elements that are not included should have been. Nor can it provide an opinion on the quality of the content. Author and peer review remain critical components of ensuring quality metadata.

It is often easier for people, as opposed to other computers, to view a more verbose rendition of the raw XML. For this purpose, XML provides style sheets that can transform an XML document into a number of other formats—another XML document, text, HTML, PDF, etc. Microsoft Internet Explorer (version 4 and higher) comes with a default XML style sheet built in. While its collapsible tree structure is useful, what it presents is still the raw XML. Metavist provides a style sheet, NBII_classic.xsl, to generate a more person-friendly display in a browser. This style sheet is provided as part of the installation. By default, when Metavist creates a metadata document, it assumes that the style sheet is in the same directory as the metadata file. Changing the location, or the style sheet reference, is discussed in the "Options menu" section (page 9 of the manual).

Installing Metavist 2005

The program requires Microsoft® Windows® 2000 or XP and the Microsoft .Net Framework version 1.1. The target display resolution is 800x600 or higher. The .Net Framework requires about 30MB of free disk space; Metavist requires about 5MB. The .Net Framework installation program comes with the program; you will need Administrator rights to successfully install it. Installation of Metavist itself does not require Administrator rights. Because Metavist was written in a .Net language, you can simply copy the executable file anywhere on your hard drive and it will run successfully. Nonetheless, installing via the setup program is recommended. The installation program will add an entry to Add/Remove Programs, put an icon on your desktop, and create an entry in the Start menu.

To install the software, first unzip the software package if necessary. Second, run Setup and follow the instructions on-screen. If Setup indicates that your machine needs the .Net Framework, the recommended approach is to exit Setup, run 'dotnetfx.exe' to install the .Net Framework, then re-run Setup to install Metavist. Alternatively, you can continue the installation and Setup will attempt to retrieve and install the 25MB .Net Framework via the Internet. Installing the .Net Framework takes a while and may require a reboot; installing Metavist is much simpler and faster. After a successful installation, the program directory (default of c:\program files\metavist) contains:

- the program file, Metavist.exe
- this manual
- PDF versions of the FGDC standard definition (FGDC 1998), the Profile definition (FGDC 1999), and the FGDC workbook (FGDC 2000)
- the XML schema for this implementation
- an XSLT style sheet for viewing NBII metadata files in a Web browser such as Microsoft Internet Explorer, version 5.0 or later
- two examples

USING METAVIST 2005

Data Format Conventions

To facilitate data entry, Metavist's user interface attempts to present data elements in commonly used formats. However, the metadata documents it creates conform to required standard formats. As specified in FGDC (1998), these formatting conventions are used in the output files:

Δ Calendar Dates (Years, Months, and Days)

- Common Era (C.E.) to December 31, 9999 C.E.—Values are formatted as YYYY for years, YYYYMM for a month of a year, and YYYYMMDD for a day of a year.

- Before Common Era (B.C.E.) to 9999 B.C.E.—Values are formatted as for Common Era dates but are preceded by "bc" (e.g., bcYYYY for years).

- Before Common Era before 9999 B.C.E.—Values consist of as many numeric characters as needed to represent the number of the year B.C.E., preceded by lower case letters "cc" (e.g., ccYYYYYY). Months and days are not relevant for this timeframe.

- Common Era after 9999 A.D.—Values consist of as many numeric characters as needed to represent number of the year C.E., preceded by the lower case letters "cd" (e.g., cdYYYYYY). Months and days are not relevant for this timeframe.

Δ Time of Day (Hours, Minutes, and Seconds)

- Because some geospatial data and related applications are sensitive to time of day information, three conventions are sanctioned. When authoring a metadata document you may choose which convention will be used, but you must use that convention throughout the document. The conventions are:
  - *Local Time*. Values follow the 24-hour timekeeping system for local time of day in the hours, minutes, seconds, and decimal fractions of a second (to the precision desired) without separators convention (general form of HHMMSSSS).

  - *Local Time with Time Differential Factor*. Values follow the 24-hour timekeeping system for local time of day in hours, minutes, seconds, and decimal fractions of a second (to the precision desired) without separators convention. This value is followed, without separators, by the time differential factor. The time differential factor expresses the difference in hours and minutes between local time and Universal Time (Greenwich Mean Time). It is represented by a four-digit number preceded by a plus sign (+) or minus sign (-), indicating that hours and minutes local time is ahead of or behind Universal Time, respectively. The general form is HHMMSSSSshhmm, where HHMMSSSS is the local time using 24-hour timekeeping, 's' is the plus or minus sign for the time differential factor, and hhmm is the time differential factor. (This option allows authors to record local time and time zone information. For example, Eastern Standard Time has a time differential factor of -0500, Central Standard Time has a time differential factor of -0600, Eastern Daylight Time has a time differential factor of -0400, and Central Daylight Time has a time differential factor of -0500.)

  - *Universal Time (Greenwich Mean Time)*. Values follow the 24-hour timekeeping system for Universal Time of day in hours, minutes, seconds, and decimal fractions of a second (expressed to the precision desired) without separators convention, with the upper case letter "Z" directly following the low-order (or extreme right hand) time element of the 24-hour clock time expression. The general form is HHMMSSSSZ, where HHMMSSSS is Universal Time using 24-hour timekeeping, and Z is the letter "Z".

Δ   Latitude and Longitude

•   Values for latitude and longitude are expressed as decimal fractions of degrees. Whole degrees of latitude are represented by a two-digit decimal number ranging from 0 through 90. Whole degrees of longitude are represented by a three-digit decimal number ranging from 0 through 180. When a decimal fraction of a degree is specified, it is separated from the whole number of degrees by a decimal point. Decimal fractions of a degree may be expressed to the precision desired.

—   Latitudes north of the Equator are specified by a plus sign (+), or by the absence of a minus sign (-), preceding the two digits designating degrees. Latitudes south of the Equator are designated by a minus sign (-) preceding the two digits designating degrees. A point on the Equator is assigned to the Northern Hemisphere.

—   Longitudes east of the prime meridian are specified by a plus sign (+), or by the absence of a minus sign (-), preceding the three digits designating degrees of longitude. Longitudes west of the meridian are designated by minus sign (-) preceding the three digits designating degrees.

A point on the prime meridian is assigned to the Eastern Hemisphere. A point on the 180th meridian is assigned to the Western Hemisphere. One exception to this last convention is permitted. For the special condition of describing a band of latitude around the Earth, the East Bounding Coordinate data element shall be assigned the value +180 (180) degrees.

—   Any spatial address with latitude of +90 (90) or -90 degrees will specify the position at the North or South Pole, respectively. The component for longitude may have any legal value.

Δ   Network Addresses and File Names

•   Values for file names, network addresses for computer systems, and related services use the Internet's Uniform Resource Locator (URL) convention when possible. The link referenced in the FGDC manual for additional details about URLs is no longer accessible. You can use your Web browser to access the URL "http://www.ling.upenn.edu/advice/url-primer.html" if you require basic information about URLs.

Design Overview

Metadata experts generally encourage incremental creation and updating of metadata throughout the course of a research project. To accommodate this approach, Metavist does not require that metadata be complete before it will save a document.

Metavist behaves like a standard Windows program. One limitation is that, like Windows Notepad, it can deal with only one document at a time. Also like Notepad, you can run more than one instance of the program at a time. Text hints and tool tips are generally available in the program (fig. 1). Tool tips are usually associated with the input boxes, not their labels. Some sections contain an additional information tab. Data entry is accomplished using standard controls such as text

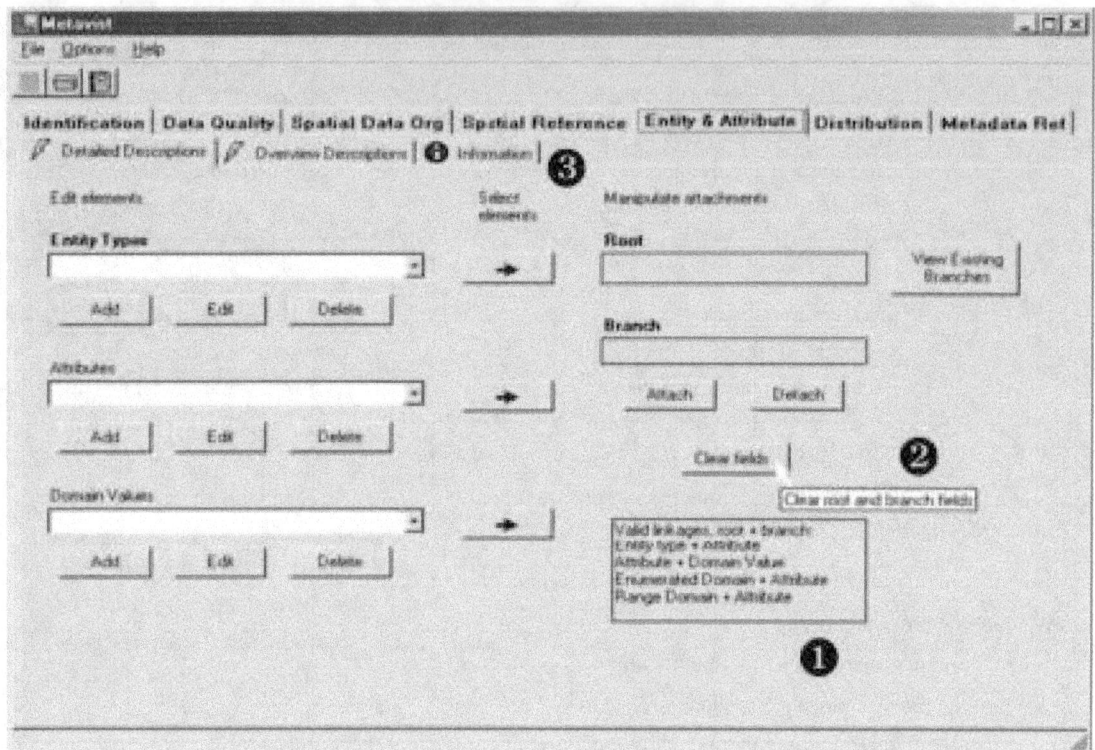

Figure 1.—On-screen help is provided via text hints (1), tool tips (2), and information tabs (3). Recall that a tooltip displays for a limited time when the mouse cursor rests on a control that has a tip associated with it. Not all controls have associated tooltips. In the example screen, the tip is associated with the 'Clear fields' button and you can see the cursor resting on the button.

boxes, numeric controls, and dropdown list boxes. Things to be aware of for these controls:

* Text boxes allow copy and paste operations both within the application and between applications. Thus, you can write longer elements in a word processor, check the grammar and spelling, and then copy the final text into Metavist. Note that special attributes like bold, italic, and superscript will not appear in the metadata output.

* You can include many special characters in your metadata by taking advantage of the Unicode character sets in Windows. The Unicode characters are easily accessed using the Character Map utility (Start…Programs…Accessories…System Tools). Some special characters do not render properly in Metavist, but do render properly when the output file is displayed in a browser.

* Numeric controls have a default number of decimal places. If you want your metadata to display fewer decimal places than generally displayed in the control, simply delete the extra digits (and the decimal point, if desired). If your metadata require more decimal places, you can enter them into the numeric field. They won't display on-screen, but will be output to the metadata file.

Clicking on the up button will increment the value by 1; the down button will decrement by 1. Continuing to press on a button will cause the appropriate action to be repeated. Similar behavior can be generated by placing the cursor in the control and pressing the up or down key. All the numeric controls have minimum and maximum values. Values you enter are checked against these bounds before metadata are written to file. If you want to force a check for a particular control, put the cursor in the appropriate field and press the Enter key.

* Generally, dropdown boxes will allow you to type in your own text to correctly describe an item not covered by the responses defined in the standard (i.e., the element's domain includes "free text"). In some cases, the standard only allows values from a certain set. For these cases, the dropdown boxes will not permit text editing.

* Some elements can have multiple entries. The entries are displayed in a list box and are manipulated using the associated Add, Edit, and Delete buttons.

* Radio buttons are used in a number of places to affect what fields are available for editing. Disabled sections are visually grayed out. (Radio buttons are shown in figure 6 where they are used to select the type of date and the type of calendar).

While a number of elements can be specified in the primary program window, many elements will generate child windows specific to the element. Drilling down to a particular element may generate as many as six windows on-screen at one time.

Menus

The File menu and the toolbar buttons (fig. 2) will let you create a new file or open an existing metadata file. Existing metadata files must be XML files having the 'xml' extension and proper formatting. Metavist creates appropriately formatted files, as does ESRI's ArcCatalog software. ArcCatalog files include additional information associated with ESRI's Profile for FGDC. This material is not read into Metavist, nor is it saved in Metavist documents. Conversely, Metavist-generated files are readable by ArcCatalog (select the FGDC XML import option), but the Biological Profile elements will not be processed.

The Help menu is limited in this version. The About item provides some basic information about the software, but the Metavist Help item only tells where additional information is located. Help is currently provided by on-screen text and tool tips. A future version of Metavist may incorporate a more comprehensive formal help system.

Figure 2.—Metavist 2005 at startup (colors will vary with system configuration).

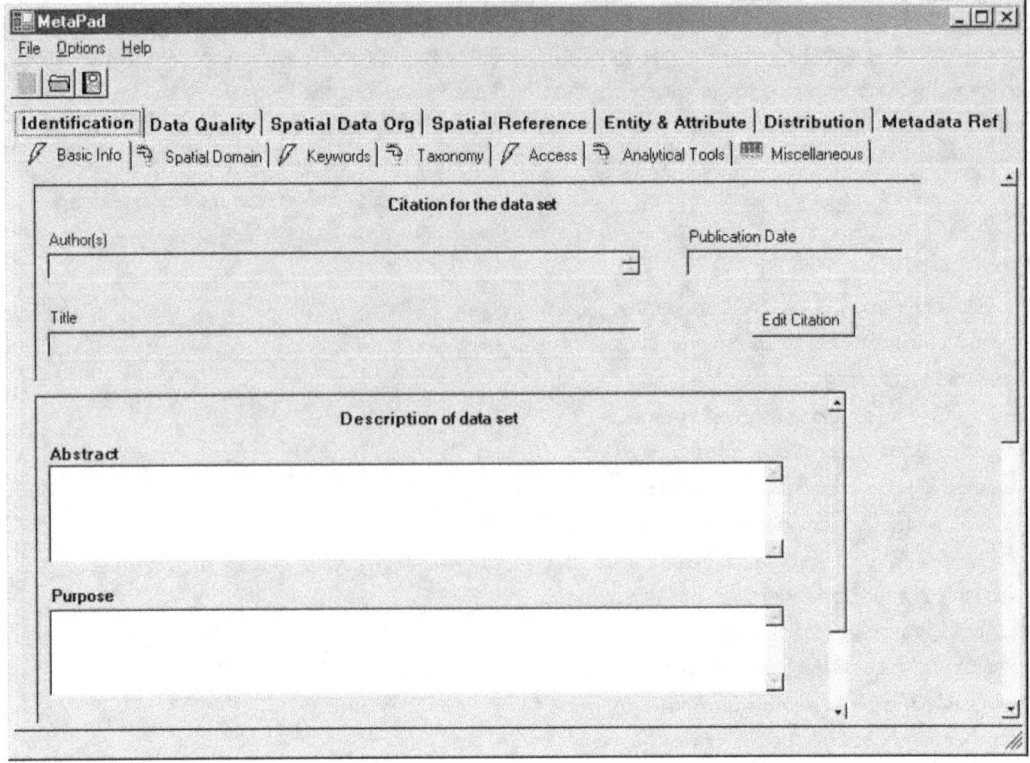

Figure 3.—A new document in Metavist 2005. Notice that the two scroll bars are at the top of their ranges, indicating the presence of additional data entry items further down in the window.

When you create a new document, the application looks like figure 3. Because Metavist works with only one document at a time, the New button has been grayed out. The Open button remains active. The Options menu and Save button have been activated, as have the Save and Save As menu items in the File menu. When the Open button, or menu item, is used to load an existing document, the program does not save existing metadata, nor does it present a "Do you want to save?" dialog box. Therefore, make sure to save the metadata before exiting if the updated version is the desired one. This approach follows the user interface structure recommended in Cooper and Riemann (2003).

When you open an existing file, which must have the extension 'xml', the program checks the content to ensure it is validly formed XML. If this is not the case, an error message appears with an explanation of the problem (fig. 4), and the program returns to its previous state. If the file is valid XML, then the contents are read into memory and the metadata elements interpreted. If an element contains content that does not match its type, the program displays an error message (fig. 5). Unless indicated otherwise, errors result in the illegal value being set to whatever the metadata standard's default value is for that element. Processing errors can take some time and this can suggest that the program has stopped

Figure 4.—Example error message when file being opened is not valid XML. The message displays what the program knows about where the XML error is.

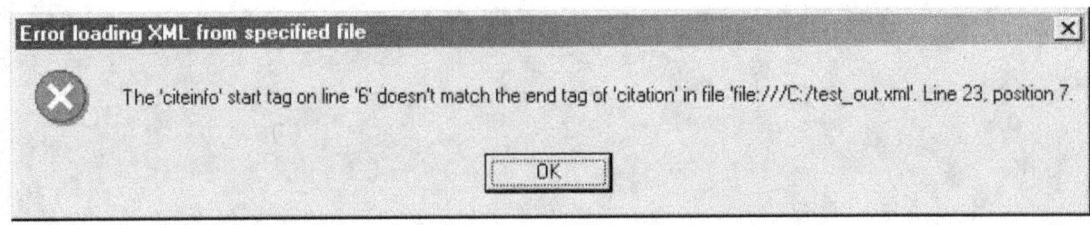

8

Distribution Information

Transfer Size of 214 megabytes could not be converted to a number.

OK

Figure 5.—Example error message when element content does not match required type. Distribution Information: Transfer Size should be a real number > 0 but the value contains the text "megabytes". The default value of '0' will be used instead of the illegal value. '214' by itself would have been valid—integers can be converted to real numbers without loss of information.

running properly. A sense for the processing time delay can be obtained by first opening the volcano atlas example (which is entirely well formed) and then the oceanography example (which generates the error described in figure 5). Depending on your system speed, the volcano atlas file should open almost immediately. The oceanography example should be noticeably slower the first time you open it.

If you close and then open the oceanography example a second time, the program will process the errors much faster. The first time the error is encountered, the program has to load error processing code; the second time the error is encountered, that error processing code is already loaded and therefore displays the error message faster than the first time. Metavist is designed to load as much of the valid metadata as it can find in the file; errors in the file should cause error messages to appear and the related metadata elements to be left blank or otherwise modified as described in the error message.

When working with metadata, the main part of the window is filled with objects (fig. 3). Under the toolbar is a set of primary tabs corresponding to the seven major stand-alone sections of the standard. Each primary tab has its own set of secondary tabs. In figure 3, the secondary tabs for Identification Information are Basic Info, Keywords, Spatial Domain, etc. The subsections generally have the same order as in the official documentation to facilitate reference to that documentation.

In addition to their titles, the secondary tabs have icons that denote whether those subsections are Mandatory (lightning bolts), Mandatory if Applicable (faucet – turn it on when needed), or Optional (birthday cake – a tasty offering to the consumer of your metadata). These icons reflect only the most demanding level of the elements on the tab. For example, a tab with a Mandatory icon may also contain main elements that are Mandatory if Applicable or Optional. Tabs with an Optional icon will not contain Mandatory or Mandatory if Applicable main elements. Labels for each data element, or group of elements, are presented in boldface, regular type, or italic. These correspond to Mandatory, Mandatory If Applicable, and Optional. Optional elements are also marked with the keyword 'optional' in parentheses by the label. Be aware that an optional compound element may contain simple elements that become mandatory once you've chosen to fill in the optional compound element. An example is Identification—Miscellaneous—Cross Reference. Providing a cross-reference citation is optional. If you choose to provide one, then providing information on the cross-reference's originators, publication date, etc. is mandatory, just as it is for any citation using the Citation Information structure.

Options menu

There are two options under the Options menu. The first option is specifying how time is represented in the metadata. By default, time is assumed to be Local, but it can be changed to Universal or Local + Differential. If you create some time elements under one time representation and then change the representation, the earlier time elements will not be correct. Although the program will warn you about the problem when you perform a save, it will complete the operation using the flawed metadata. When a metadata file is read into the software, the time convention element (Metadata Reference Information Section) is read first to set the time option. The program does attempt to format time elements encountered in the rest of the metadata according to the option specified in the time convention element. If no time convention element is present, then any time elements encountered will be formatted using the default Local time option.

The second option is specifying the name of the file containing the style sheet used to display the metadata in a browser (so this style sheet reformats the XML as HTML in browsers such as Internet Explorer and Mozilla that understand this XML processing instruction). By default, the file 'NBII_classic.xsl' is used. This style sheet is based on the "classic" style sheet used by ESRI and FGDC to display FGDC metadata, but enhanced to handle the additional elements in NBII metadata.

The lack of path information in the default style sheet name means that the style sheet file must be in the same directory as the metadata file to view the formatted metadata in a browser window. If you select 'New URL', you can either type in a file name (and path, if relevant) or use the Browse button to find the file of interest. If the URL is set to an Internet URL, then the metadata will only display successfully when the computer is connected to the Internet. If you set this option to 'No style sheet', Internet Explorer (5.0 and later) will use its internal style sheet to render the XML (color coded, tags visible and collapsible). Behavior in other browsers will vary; some will simply refuse to display the metadata at all.

Saving metadata

Use the File menu or keyboard shortcuts to invoke the standard Save or Save As dialog box. The Save button will either save to the existing file name or invoke the Save As dialog if the metadata document doesn't have a name yet. In Metavist 2005, metadata files are always saved with the 'xml' extension and are written in XML that conforms to the schema that accompanies the software. Elements that lack an entry but are known to always be required are given an attribute that displays a reminder in red print when viewed in a browser using the NBII_classic style sheet. Elements that lack an entry even though required in the particular instance are simply output with a blank entry. For example, in the Browse Graphic element of the Identification Information section, if

the file name and file type are present but not the file description, then the file description is output with a blank entry.

When you've completed a set of metadata, you can exit the program in any of the usual ways or go to File...Close to close the current metadata file and be able to start a new one. It is important to be aware that simply closing a file does **not** save the metadata, nor does the program present a "Do you want to save?" dialog box. Similarly, exiting the program neither saves the current metadata nor presents a confirmation dialog box. This follows recommended interface design (Cooper and Reimann 2003).

With the program basics covered, let's discuss some aspects of processing metadata that are not apparent from the program interface. This discussion will be organized by section.

Section 1. Identification Information

Time Period of Content (Basic Info tab)

In the Time Period Information subsection of this element (use the scroll bar on the right hand side of the window to bring this section into view), the program has a number of conventions for handling Gregorian dates. These are described below in the three date handling lists. The conventions listed under "Date handling when working inside the program" are also relevant for Geologic Ages dates.

Date handling when reading a file:
- If a Single Date/Time has Unknown as the date value, the program selects the Unknown radio button (fig. 6).
- If a Single Date/Time in Multiple Dates/Times has Unknown as its date value, that date is ignored. If ignoring these dates results in only one date/time being entered, the program will downgrade from 'Multiple dates' to 'A single date'. If it results in no dates being entered, then the program will select the Unknown radio button.
- If either the beginning or ending date in Range of Dates/Times has Unknown as its date value, the entire range is treated as unknown.
- Any time entry that has Unknown as its value is ignored (since it is an optional element).

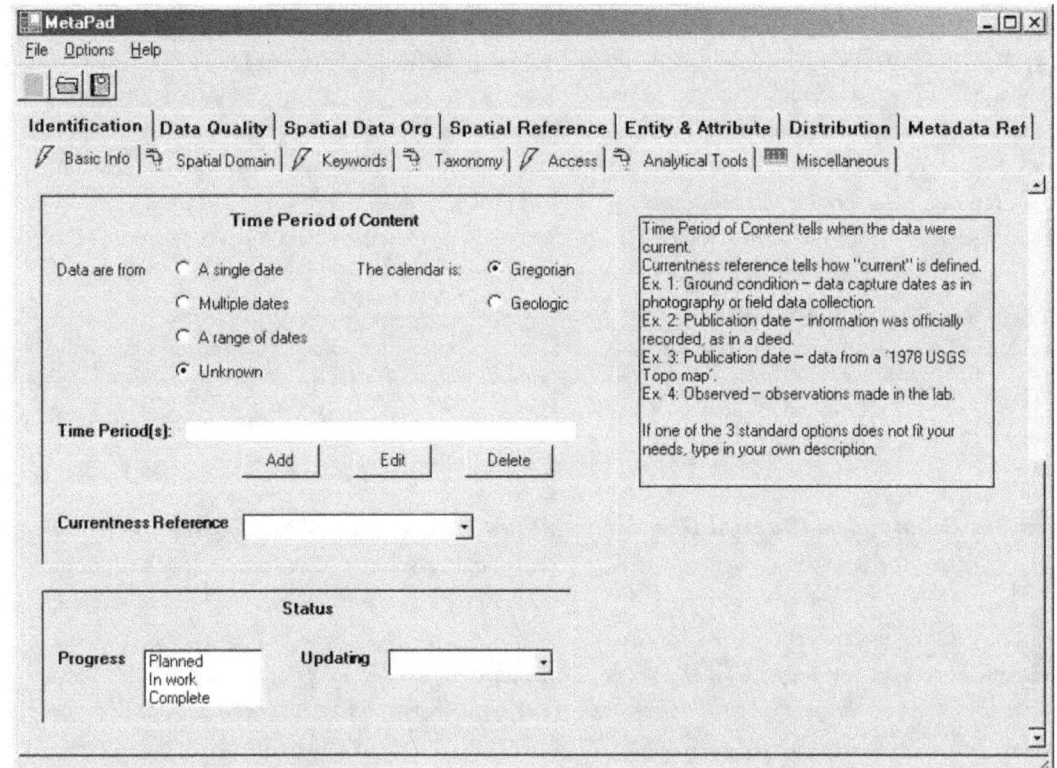

Date handling when working inside the program:

- Changing the selection from Single, Multiple, or Range to Unknown also clears all entered dates and times.
- Changing the selection from Single to Multiple has no effect on the dates/times; changing from Single to Range sets the Single value as both the beginning date and the ending date. Editing this to create a proper range is encouraged.
- Changing the selection from Multiple to Single retains only the first of the multiple dates/times; changing from Multiple to Range sets the first of the multiple dates as the beginning date, and the last of the multiple dates as the ending date. This result will sometimes require editing to have the proper values anchoring the range.
- Changing the selection from Range to Single sets the beginning date as the single date; changing from Range to Multiple sets the beginning date and the ending date as the first two entries in the multiple date collection.

Date handling when saving a file:

- Errors in associating day of month to month are not checked in this version of the software. So it is possible to put February 30 in the date field. This flexibility will probably be reduced in future versions of the software.
- If there is only one date/time in the collection, it is output as a Single Date/Time, regardless of the radio button selection.
- For Range, the program does **not** verify that beginning date is earlier than ending date when reading or saving a document. Ranges that are created in the program are required to have proper date structure, but errors introduced via an input file will be retained unless the range is edited in Metavist. Proper date structure is defined to include the trivially correct case of the beginning date and ending date being the same. Time, if you provide it, is not checked.
- If the Unknown radio button is selected, then a Range will be written to the file with the beginning and ending dates having the Unknown value. This is done because Time Period of Content is a mandatory element and most data sets are collected over a period of time.

- If the Unknown radio button is not selected, but there are no dates in the collection, then the program acts as though the Unknown radio button was selected.

The Currentness Reference for the oceanography example illustrates poor form for this element. While Metavist will let you type in a single line of similar length, this type of information is better suited to the Source Citation in Lineage (Data Quality Information). A more appropriate choice would have been "ground condition".

Data Set G-polygons (Spatial Domain tab)

If you are describing the polygons with G-ring points, Metavist reminds you to enter at least three points and that closing the polygon will be done automatically. This closure is implicit. So while the metadata document will contain all the required points, the data entry display lacks the closing point.

Taxonomic Classification (Taxonomy tab)

In the Taxonomy subsection, the Taxonomic Classification requires a technical description of the species covered by the data set (example in table 1). If you need help with the technical description, there is a link in the Add Child and Edit windows to the Integrated Taxonomic Information System (ITIS) Web site run by USDA. These windows also have a supplemental information tab with a description of how to use ITIS.

If you read the formal documentation for the standard, you might have some difficulty figuring out how to describe multiple species if those species reside in multiple Kingdoms. The program provides a cheat for your use. Metavist defines a new taxonomic rank called Empire (it's at the top of the dropdown list of defined rank names). Empire has only one taxonomic rank value, Biovitae (Latin, more or less, for 'biological life'), and one associated common name ('carbon-based life forms'). These are automatically filled in when you choose the Empire rank name. You can attach as many Kingdoms to Empire as needed.

Point of Contact (Access tab)

The standard specifies that each line of an address resides in its own Address element. The oceanography example contains an error in the structure of the Contact Address—a multi-line address in the Address element. Metavist reads this incorrect format successfully. If the metadata are saved, they are written correctly without any user intervention.

Analytical Tool (Analytical Tools tab)

The main concept to keep in mind with this element is that it references tools that are "intrinsically bound" to the data set. Basic data containers (e.g., spreadsheets or databases) and standard analysis tools (e.g., statistical or GIS software) don't fall into the category. An example of an analytical tool is a specialized meteorological model—the data being analyzed are heavily manipulated versions of raw data, and an average researcher could not recreate the data used in the analysis without recourse to the specialized tool(s) used to process the raw observations.

Table 1.—Taxonomic Classification for "red maple" or *Acer rubrum var. rubrum* reproduced from FGDC (1999)

Taxon rank name	Taxon rank value	Applicable common names
Kingdom	Plantae	plants
Division	Magnoliaphyta	
Class	Magnoliopsida	
Subclass	Rosidae	
Order	Sapindales	
Family	Aceraceae	maples
Genus	Acer	maples
Species	*Acer rubrum var. rubrum*	red maple

Browse Graphics (Miscellaneous tab)

The FGDC spatial data standard defines these as static pictures in formats such as JPEG and GIF. The Biological Profile allows other types of files for describing the data set, including audio and video file types. These files may describe study sites, data collection methods, and other related information. Also note that this set of elements simply describes the browse graphic—the graphic is not included with the metadata. While the Browse Graphic File Name element is free text, a URL pointing to the location of the browse graphic can be specified.

Cross Reference (Miscellaneous tab)

Formally, the Cross Reference element provides citations for related data sets. It also seems reasonable to provide citations to papers that cited the data set.

Section 2. Data Quality Information

When saving metadata to file, this section is processed only if at least one of the three mandatory elements contains content. Thus, the program checks the Logical Consistency Report and Completeness Report for the presence of text, and then checks for the presence of at least one Process Step (Lineage tab). If any of these are true, then the whole collection of elements is evaluated. If none of these are true, then none of the section is saved—even if some non-mandatory elements are present. For the case in which at least one of the reports contains text but no Process Steps were described, when the metadata document is saved Metavist provides a default Process Step: Process Description = "No process steps have been described for this data set" and Process Date = "Unknown".

In the Lineage subsection, the program does not enforce the rule that Citation Abbreviations used in Process Steps must be defined in a Source Information entry. This is done to facilitate episodic creation of metadata. Process Steps with real or placeholder Citation Abbreviations can be created during the analysis process, and then cleaned up and augmented with Source Information at a later time.

In the Source Information subsection of Lineage, the rules for Time Period of Content are the same as for the comparable collection of elements in the Identification Information section. What differs is that you are describing data you used but which was collected and made available to you by others.

Section 3. Spatial Data Organization Information

In 'Point and Vector Object Information', the maximum value for the optional 'Point and Vector Object Count' element is currently 1 million. In 'Raster Object Information', the maximum value for the optional '*type* Count' elements is currently 1 billion.

Section 4. Spatial Reference Information

Horizontal Coordinate System Definition

The Geographic and Local definition elements are straightforward. Here are some tips for dealing with Planar definitions:

- **Map Projections and Grid Systems**—When working in the Parameters window, the only controls enabled are those used by the particular projection. These controls also have a check mark in the checkbox at their left. If you uncheck the box, that parameter will be assigned a blank value in the output file, rather than whatever happens to be in the control when you click OK in the Planar Parameters window. The one exception to this rule is for projections that can specify 1 or 2 Standard Parallel values. If the check box for the **second** Standard Parallel is unchecked, then the output file simply does not contain an entry for the second Standard Parallel. However, if you later edit the parameters you will need to uncheck the box again.
- **Map Projections**—False Easting and False Northing are arbitrarily bounded at ±500 million; Scale Factor elements at 500.
- **Map projection: Space Oblique Mercator**— Landsat Number has a maximum value of 50; Path Number has a maximum value of 500.

Because these bounds are much larger than current actual values for these parameters, it is not difficult to provide incorrect information on these elements in the metadata.

- **Map projection: Other**—If you need to describe a map projection other than one of the 21 projections defined by the metadata standard, click on Add User-Defined Projection Type to provide a name to the new projection. This name will be added to the list of options and automatically chosen as the projection to work with. Then click on Edit Parameters to provide a written description of the projection.
- **Grid coordinate system: Universal Polar Stereographic (UPS)**—One of the UPS Zone Identifiers must be highlighted. Scrolling through the list and stopping at the correct identifier is not sufficient; the correct identifier must be clicked on to select it.
- **Grid coordinate system: State Plane Coordinate System**—Zone Identifier is specified using a numeric control that constrains values to four-digit numbers. Therefore, Zone Identifiers that contain leading zeros will not show those leading zeros during editing. However, the leading

zeros are added to the values before metadata are written to file.

In the Geodetic Model subsection, default values for Semi-major Axis and Denominator of Flattening Ratio are provided. Therefore, if you want this collection of elements to appear in the metadata output, you need to specify the Ellipsoid Name.

Section 5. Entity and Attribute Information

Although the icons on both the Detailed Descriptions tab and the Overview Descriptions tab suggest that both subsections are mandatory, the actual rule is to choose one, the other, or both. When describing data that do not have a geospatial component, it is probably easier to use the Overview Description than the Detailed Description.

Detailed Description

Detailed Description (fig. 7) is probably the most complex part of the metadata standard, and its tab has the least intuitive layout. The dropdown boxes contain lists of their respective elements (Entity Types, Attributes, and Domain Values). The Add, Edit, and Delete buttons behave just as they do in other parts of

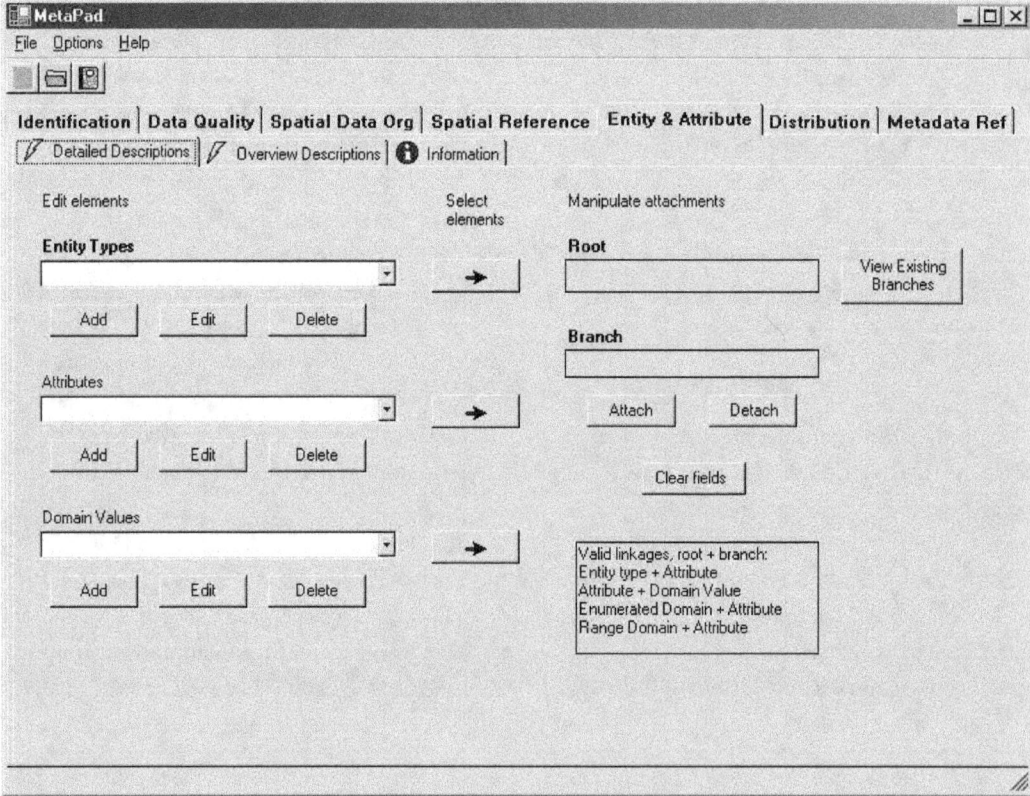

Figure 7.—The Entity & Attribute: Detailed Descriptions controls.

14

the program. The complexity is in linking the pieces to create the Detailed Descriptions. The Information tab contains a brief summary of how to do this, but a detailed guide is provided below.

The arrow button to the right of each element type will post the selected element to the "Manipulate attachments" section. The eligibility rules for posting in Root and Branch are shown at the bottom of the "Manipulate attachments" section (fig. 7). The placement rules are:

Element: Entity Type
   Rule: Always post to Root, even if another object is already present.

Element: Attribute
   Rule: Post to Root if empty.
   Rule: Post to Branch if Root is filled but Branch is empty.
   Rule: If Root and Branch are filled, display error message.

Element: Domain Value
   Rule: Enumerated and Range—post to Root if it is empty, otherwise post to Branch even if another object is already present.
   Rule: Codeset and Unrepresentable— always post to Branch, even if another object is already present.

When there is an element displayed in Root, pressing the View Existing Branches button will display the elements currently attached to the Root element. This can be helpful for ensuring that all the branches that are supposed to be attached to root have been. When there are appropriate elements displayed in Root and Branch, pressing the Attach button will graft the branch to the root. Similarly, pressing the Detach button will sever the branch from the root. These changes are reflected in the View Existing Branches display immediately. Detaching a branch does not, however, remove it from the relevant element list. There are two reasons for this behavior. First, when creating the Detailed Descriptions you can attach a branch to more than one root, so the detached branch may be required for a different root. Second, the order of branches displayed in View Existing Branches is the same as the order the branches will appear in the metadata output. By detaching and re-attaching, you can alter the display order. For example, you might want descriptions of valid attribute values to precede descriptions of codes for missing data. When work on a root/branch pair is completed, pressing 'Clear fields' will clear the Root and Branch fields.

Step by step: top-down approach

Step 1. Define the entities, attributes, and domain values.
Step 2. Place an entity into Root, place an attribute into Branch, and click Attach.
Step 3. Click 'Clear fields'.
Step 4. Repeat steps 2 and 3 for each attribute of each entity.
Step 5. Place an attribute into Root, place a domain value into Branch, and click Attach.
Step 6. If additional domain values are to be associated with the attribute, place each one into Branch and click Attach. 'Clear fields' between these steps is not necessary.
Step 7. Repeat steps 5 and 6 for each attribute.

If the steps are reversed, first attaching domain values to attributes then attaching attributes to entities, the resulting metadata structure is the same. Defining of entities, attributes, and domain values can be done as needed; these objects can also be edited after being attached and the updated information will be incorporated into the saved metadata without additional action.

Two examples

As the entity-attribute-domain value structure may be unfamiliar, here are two examples.

Example 1.

Entity: person
    Attribute: sex
        Enumerated Domain value: male
        Enumerated Domain value: female
    Attribute: income
        Range Domain value: $0 to $1 million
        Enumerated Domain value: > $1 million
        Enumerated Domain value: not available

Example 2.

Entity: person
    Attribute: income
        Range Domain value: $3000 to $95000
    Attribute: sex
        Enumerated Domain value: male
          Attribute: prostate cancer
            Enumerated Domain value: yes
            Enumerated Domain value:
                treated successfully
            Enumerated Domain value: no
        Enumerated Domain value: female
          Attribute: number of pregnancies
            Enumerated Domain values: 0,
              1, 2, 3, 4, 5+

Multiple occurrences of domain values and attributes

As noted above, you can attach a given branch to more than one root. For example, the volcano example uses the Unrepresentable Domain "Numbers for the features." in multiple attributes. When creating metadata, you can create this domain definition once and re-use it as many times as needed, and it will only appear in the Domain Values list only once. When reading metadata into the program from a file, if multiple attributes have the same Codeset Domain or Unrepresentable Domain, they will reference a single entry in the Domain Value dropdown list. However, if multiple attributes have the same Enumerated Domain or Range Domain, those attributes will reference different entries in the Domain Value dropdown list. Because these two domain types can accept additional attributes, the software does not attempt to compare a new domain being read in to the domains already read in.

Re-used attributes behave like Enumerated Domains. When you are creating metadata, you can create the attribute definition once and re-use it as many times as needed, and it will appear in the Attributes list only once. However, when reading metadata from a file, each instance of the attribute will generate an entry in the dropdown list.

Editing attributes and domain values

When editing an Attribute, you will see a dropdown list for Attribute Domain Values (fig. 8). This list is not editable; it simply shows what Domain Values are currently assigned to the Attribute, just as View Existing Branches does from the main window.

Suppose you want to describe Attribute Value Accuracy Information, but need to deal with an attribute that does not have a numeric value. In this case, set the required numeric accuracy to be some arbitrary value other than 0.00, and provide the text description of accuracy in the Attribute Value Accuracy Explanation. If Attribute Value Accuracy is set to 0.00, the program assumes that these optional elements should not be included in the output.

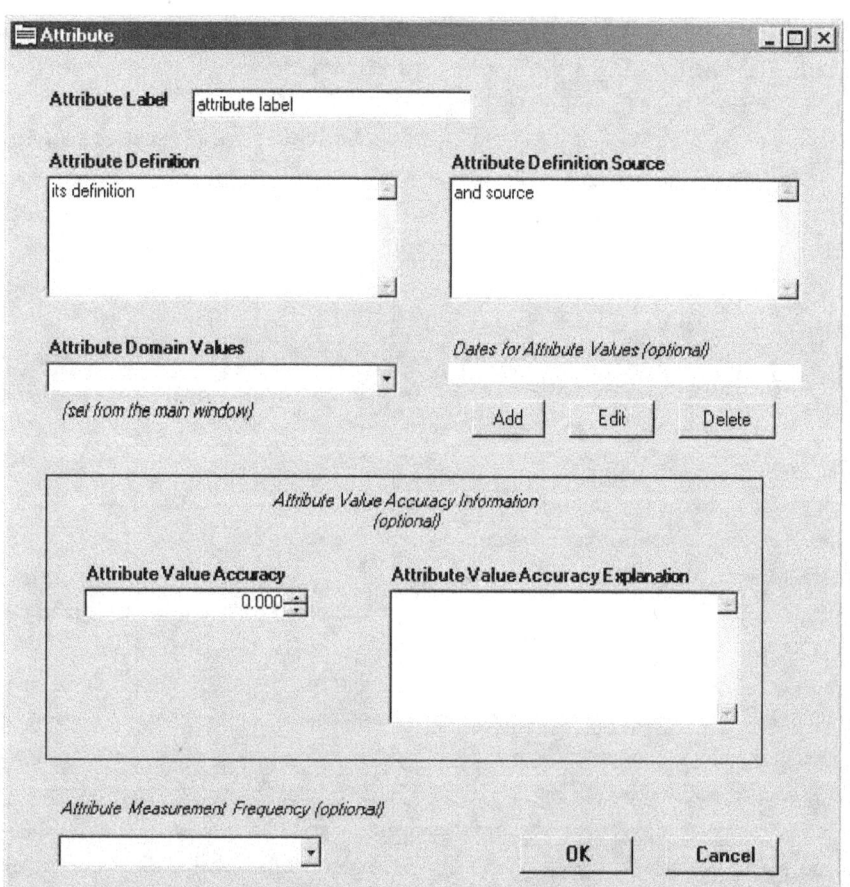

Figure 8.—The Attribute
description window.

When describing Attribute Domain Values, there is a disagreement between the written standard and the graphical rendition. The written standard specifies that there is at most one Enumerated Domain, with an unlimited number of Enumerated Domain Values beneath it. The graphical rendition shows an unlimited number of Enumerated Domains, each with at most one Enumerated Domain Value. Metavist implements the standard according to the graphical rendition. Judging from the construction of their XSLT style sheet, and the volcano metadata file, this is also how ESRI implements the standard. The volcano atlas example shows a number of ways that enumerated domains can be described. The oceanography example offers another approach to enumerated domains that Metavist is able to create.

Section 6. Distribution Information

When a Distributor is added or edited, a Distribution Information window is drawn with tabs for information about the Distributor, Ordering, and Prerequisites. This is the only window that has its Okay and Cancel buttons on an isolated tab. While the Distributor is mandatory if Distribution Information is to be included in the metadata, the information on the other tabs is not. Putting the OK and Cancel buttons on their own tab is designed to provide a subtle reminder to enter any appropriate information in those other tabs before returning to the main window.

There are a few additional issues to be aware of in this section, all dealing with the Digital Form for a Standard Order Process. The Digital Form data entry window can be generated by adding a Distributor, selecting the Ordering tab, adding a Standard Order Process, selecting the Digital radio button for format, and adding a Digital Form. The issues are:

- The standard specifies that if Format is present then either Format Version Number or Format Version Date must also be present. ESRI's metadata frequently do not follow this rule. To avoid losing the information provided by ESRI in the Format Specification element, Metavist fills the Format Version Number element with the value "see Format Specification" when necessary.

- The mandatory if applicable element File Decompression Technique defaults to the value "No compression applied". If you do not want this element to appear, simply delete the text from the box.

- The oceanography example contains an error in the Transfer Size element. The element is supposed to contain a real value > 0 that describes the size of the file in megabytes. The oceanography example contains the value "214 megabytes" for two of its Digital Forms. Metavist does not attempt to parse values that cannot be converted to numbers.

- Metavist deviates from the standard by not providing any capability to describe Dialup Instructions in the Online Option is not available in Metavist. Dialing into a machine is very rare in today's Web-oriented environment and this collection of elements is slated for elimination in the new international spatial metadata standard.

- The volcano example contains an unusual use of Offline Media in the Offline Option subsection (drill down to the example's Digital Form window then click the Edit button associated with Digital Transfer Option). If you need to describe such a situation, it is better form to simply set Offline Media to be "CD-ROM" and place other information into the Compatibility Information element.

Section 7. Metadata Reference Information

Metadata dates (Metadata information tab)

These elements are specified user calendar controls. When you click on the dropdown a navigable month-based calendar appears, from which you can choose the date of interest. The Metadata Review Date and Metadata Future Review Date elements become available for editing when you choose to check the box by the appropriate element name. Metavist does not check that review date is later than creation date, nor that future review date is later than review date.

Metadata Time Convention element

There is no data entry component associated with this mandatory if applicable element. Instead, when saving a metadata document Metavist determines whether a time element is used in the metadata. If there is at least one, then the program creates this element and sets its value to the currently selected time convention (local, local + differential, or universal). The time convention option was described previously.

Metadata extensions

Metavist 2005 is not extension-aware. Therefore, there is no ability to specify online linkages or profile names other than the Biological Profile. As noted earlier, this means that ESRI profile elements will not be read into Metavist, nor will they be saved in Metavist-generated files.

Technical Support

If you have questions, comments, or suggestions about the software or the manual, please direct an e-mail to drugg@fs.fed.us.

ACKNOWLEDGMENTS

Many thanks to those who reviewed this manual and the software; your contributions were invaluable in improving the quality of the final product. Special thank you's to Dr. Linda Donoghue, Station Director, and (posthumously) Dr. David Shriner, Assistant Director for Research. Linda and Dave were key forces in initiating and nurturing the data archiving program at the Station, which resulted in the creation of this software.

LITERATURE CITED

Cooper, Alan; Reimann, Robert. 2003.
About Face 2.0: the essentials of interaction design. Indianapolis,
IN: Wiley Publishing. 540 p.

ESRI. 2003.
ESRI Data & Maps 2002. Redlands, CA: ESRI. CD 2 of 8.

Federal Geographic Data Committee. 1998.
*Content standard for digital geospatial metadata (revised June
1998).* FGDC-STD-001-1998. Washington, DC: Federal Geographic
Data Committee. 90 p.

Federal Geographic Data Committee. 2000.
Content Standard for Digital Geospatial Metadata Workbook
Version 2.0. Washington, DC: Federal Geographic Data Committee.
126 p.

FGDC Biological Data Working Group and
USGS Biological Resources Division. 1999.
*Content standard for digital geospatial metadata – Biological Data
Profile.* FGDC-STD-001.1-1999. Washington, DC: Federal
Geographic Data Committee. 58 p.

APPENDIX A

Colorized Version of Metadata Standard, FGDC-STD-001.1-1999
Content Standard for Digital Geospatial Metadata, 1998
Part 1: Biological Data Profile, 1999

This color-coded graphical overview shows the organization of all the elements, their optionality, and presence in both the NBII and FGDC Standards or just the NBII Standard. The graphics for sections 1, 2, 6, 8, 9, and 10 plus the extended elements are TIF images available at the NBII Web site (http://www.nbii.gov/datainfo/metadata/standards/index.html). The graphics for sections 3, 4, 5, and 7 are GIF images available at the NBII Web site.

The graphic titled "Biological Data Profile Extended Elements" has three color-coding errors (Metavist is correctly coded.):

- In "ASCII File Structure", "Authentication" is shown as optional. It is actually mandatory if applicable.
- In "ASCII File Structure", "Quote Character" is shown as optional. It is actually mandatory if applicable.
- In "Geologic Age", "Geologic Citation" is shown as mandatory. It is actually optional.

Section 1

Identification Information

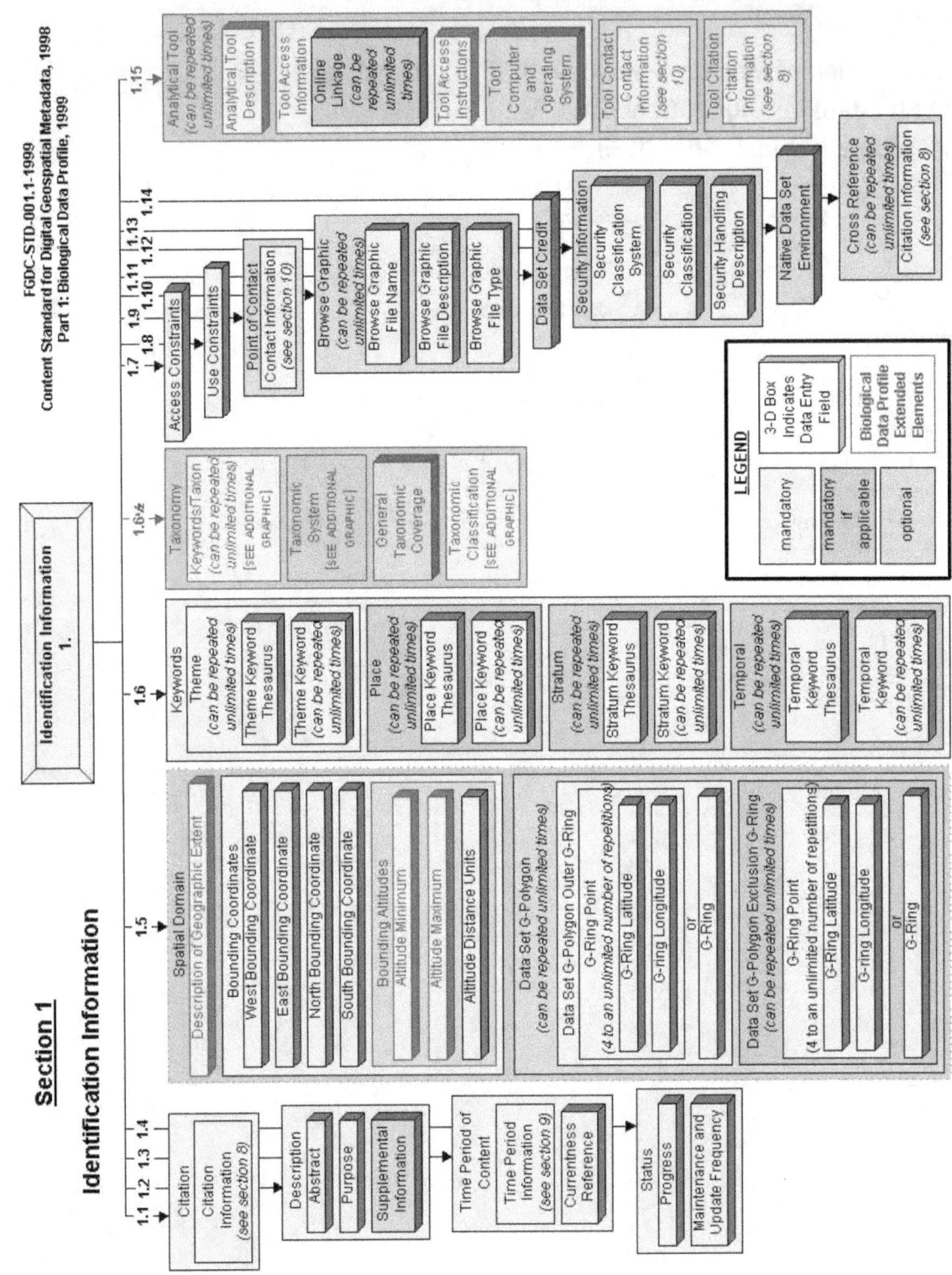

Section 2

Data Quality Information

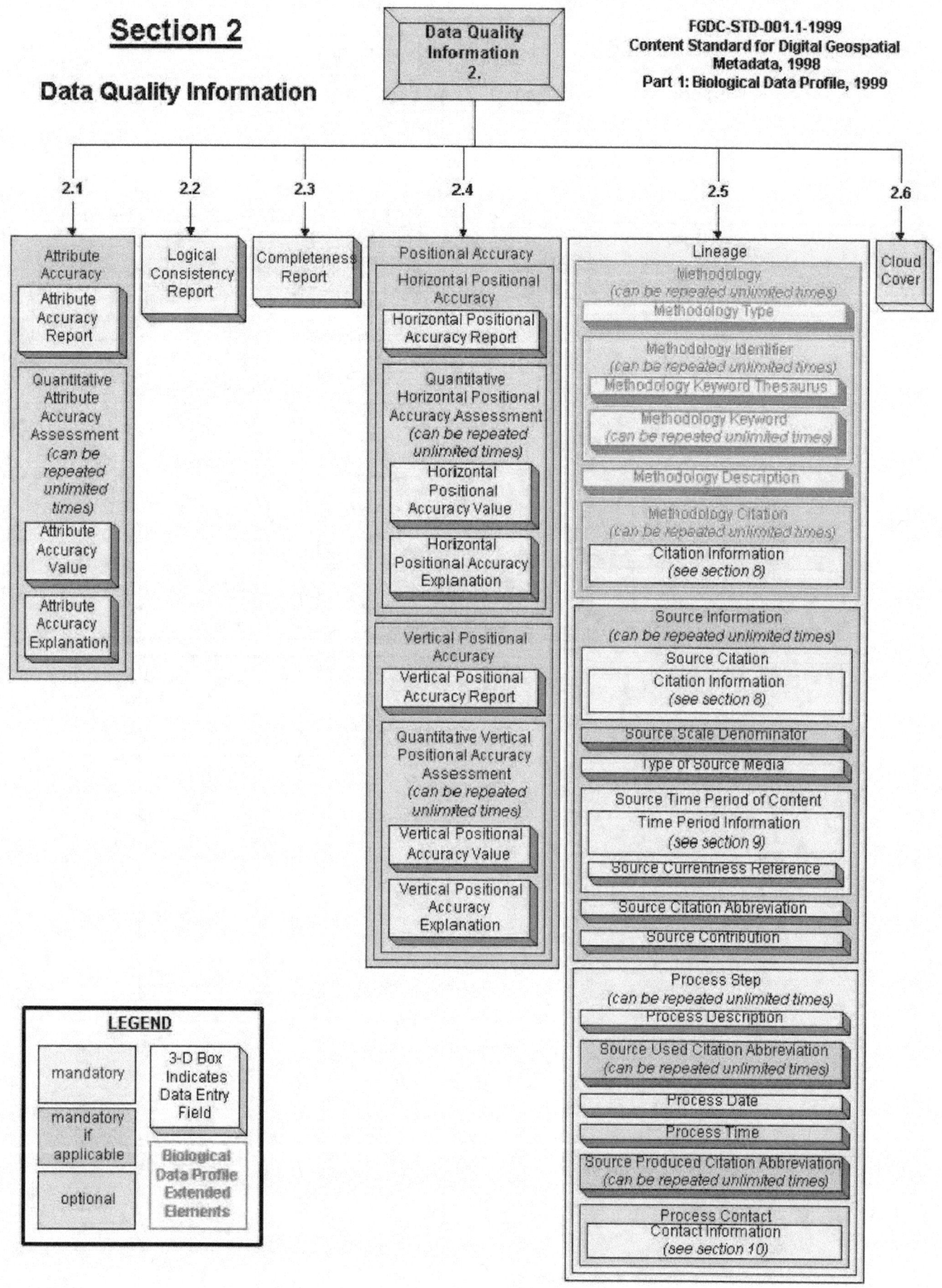

FGDC-STD-001.1-1999
Content Standard for Digital Geospatial
Metadata, 1998
Part 1: Biological Data Profile, 1999

Data Quality Information 2.

2.1 Attribute Accuracy
- Attribute Accuracy Report
- Quantitative Attribute Accuracy Assessment *(can be repeated unlimited times)*
  - Attribute Accuracy Value
  - Attribute Accuracy Explanation

2.2 Logical Consistency Report

2.3 Completeness Report

2.4 Positional Accuracy
- Horizontal Positional Accuracy
  - Horizontal Positional Accuracy Report
  - Quantitative Horizontal Positional Accuracy Assessment *(can be repeated unlimited times)*
    - Horizontal Positional Accuracy Value
    - Horizontal Positional Accuracy Explanation
- Vertical Positional Accuracy
  - Vertical Positional Accuracy Report
  - Quantitative Vertical Positional Accuracy Assessment *(can be repeated unlimited times)*
    - Vertical Positional Accuracy Value
    - Vertical Positional Accuracy Explanation

2.5 Lineage
- Methodology *(can be repeated unlimited times)*
  - Methodology Type
  - Methodology Identifier *(can be repeated unlimited times)*
    - Methodology Keyword Thesaurus
    - Methodology Keyword *(can be repeated unlimited times)*
  - Methodology Description
  - Methodology Citation *(can be repeated unlimited times)*
    - Citation Information *(see section 8)*
- Source Information *(can be repeated unlimited times)*
  - Source Citation
    - Citation Information *(see section 8)*
  - Source Scale Denominator
  - Type of Source Media
  - Source Time Period of Content
    - Time Period Information *(see section 9)*
  - Source Currentness Reference
  - Source Citation Abbreviation
  - Source Contribution
- Process Step *(can be repeated unlimited times)*
  - Process Description
  - Source Used Citation Abbreviation *(can be repeated unlimited times)*
  - Process Date
  - Process Time
  - Source Produced Citation Abbreviation *(can be repeated unlimited times)*
  - Process Contact
    - Contact Information *(see section 10)*

2.6 Cloud Cover

LEGEND

mandatory	3-D Box Indicates Data Entry Field
mandatory if applicable	Biological Data Profile Extended Elements
optional	

23

Section 3

Spatial Data Organization Information

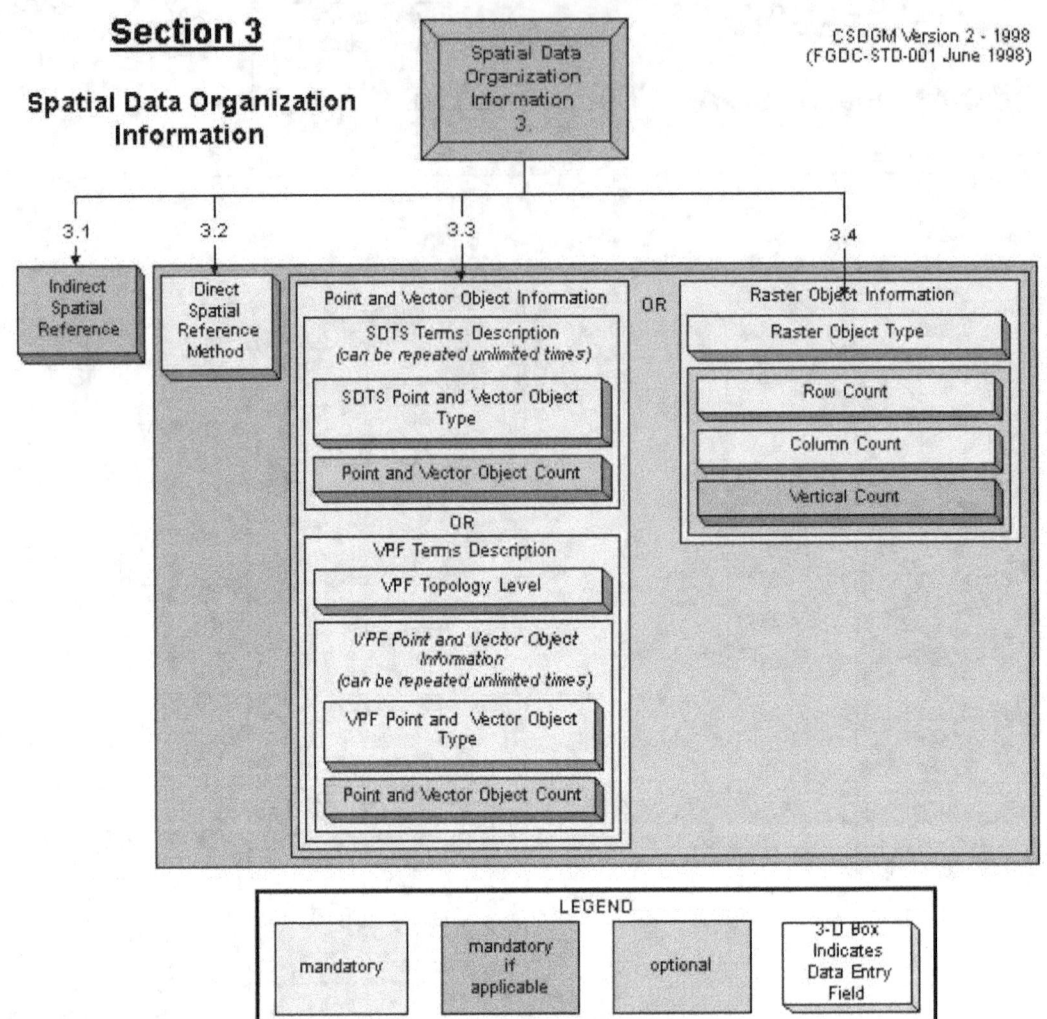

LEGEND

| mandatory | mandatory if applicable | optional | 3-D Box Indicates Data Entry Field |

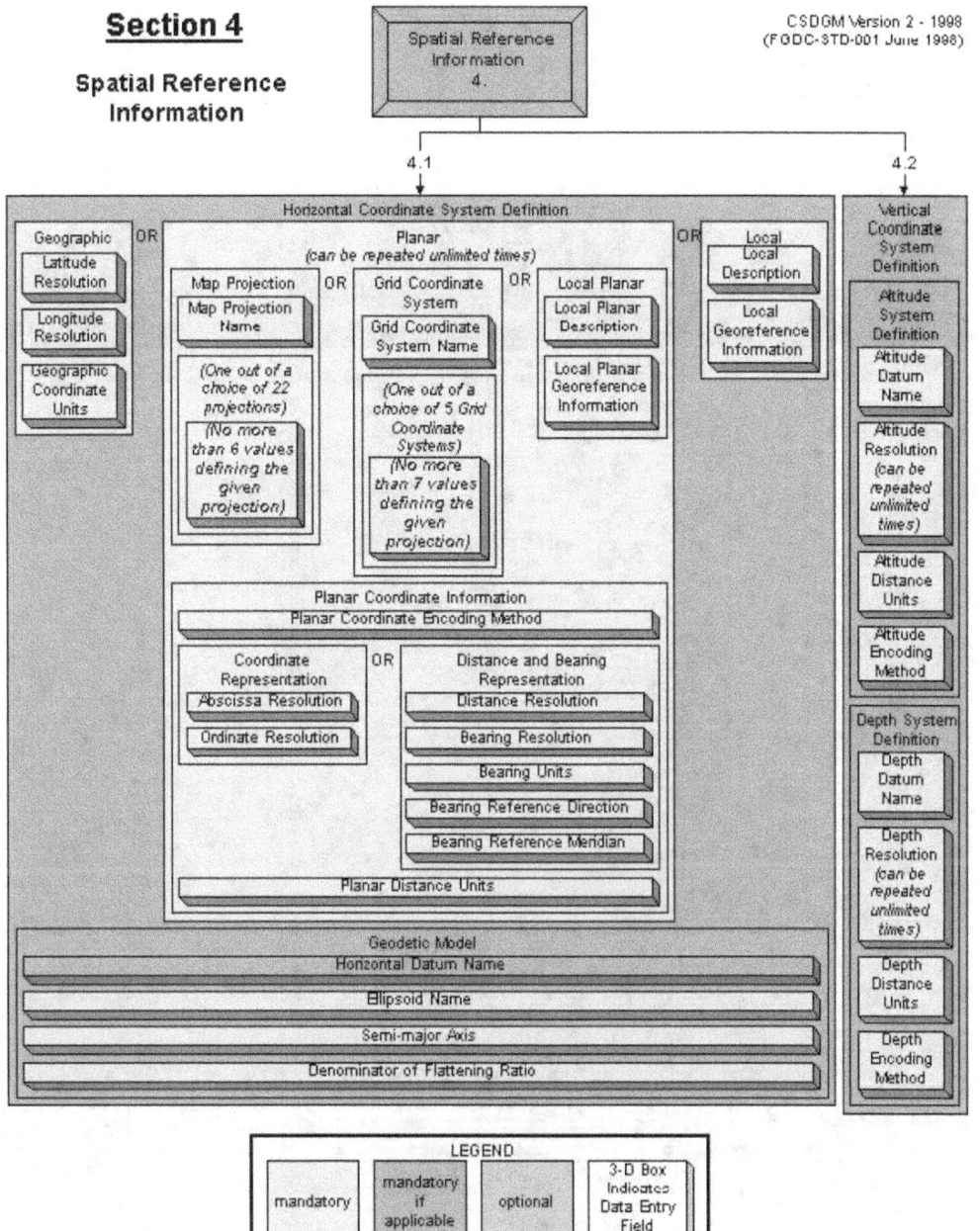

CSDGM Version 2 - 1998
(FGDC-STD-001 June 1998)

CSDGM Version 2 - 1998
(FGDC-STD-001 June 1998)

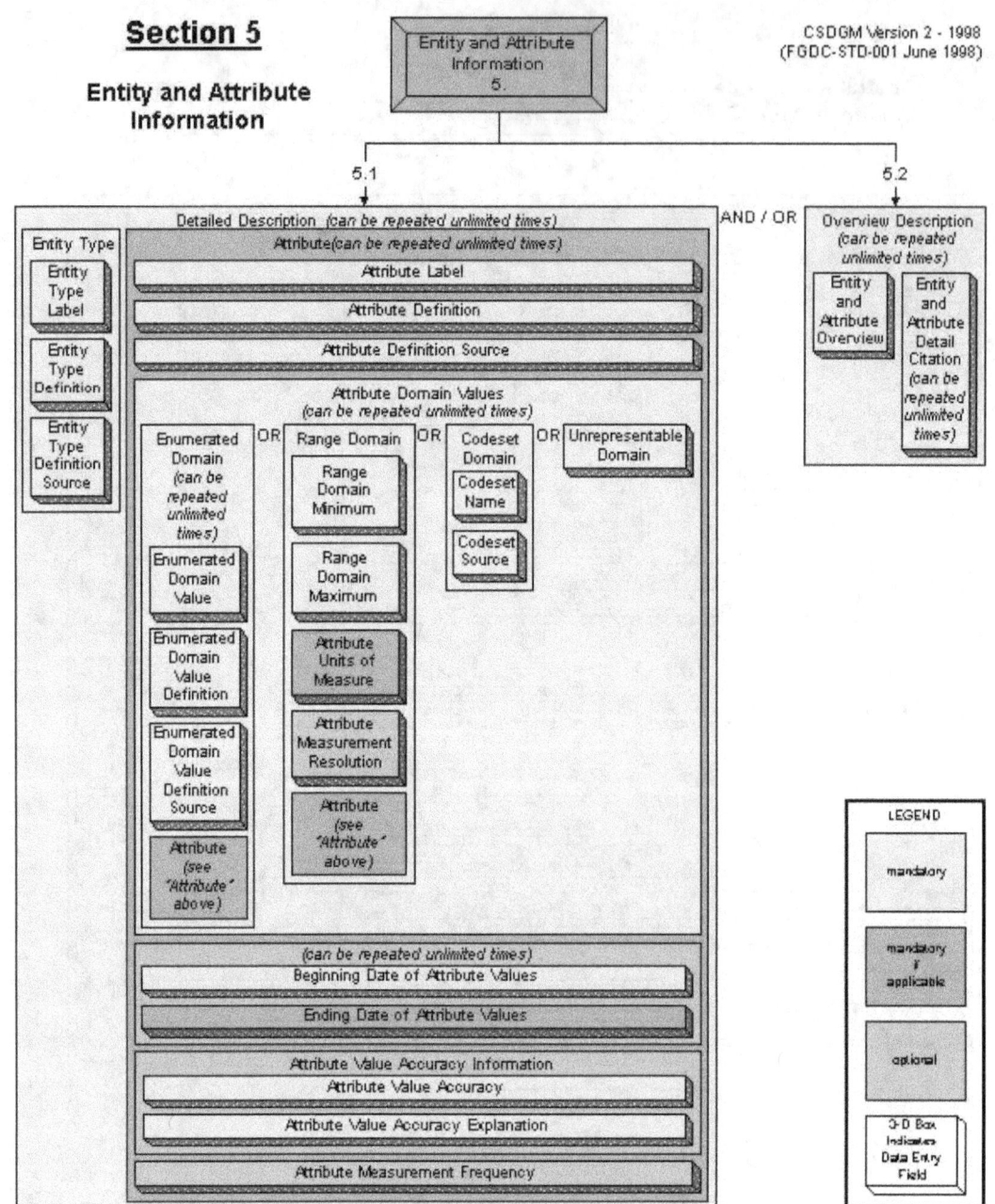

Section 6

Distribution Information

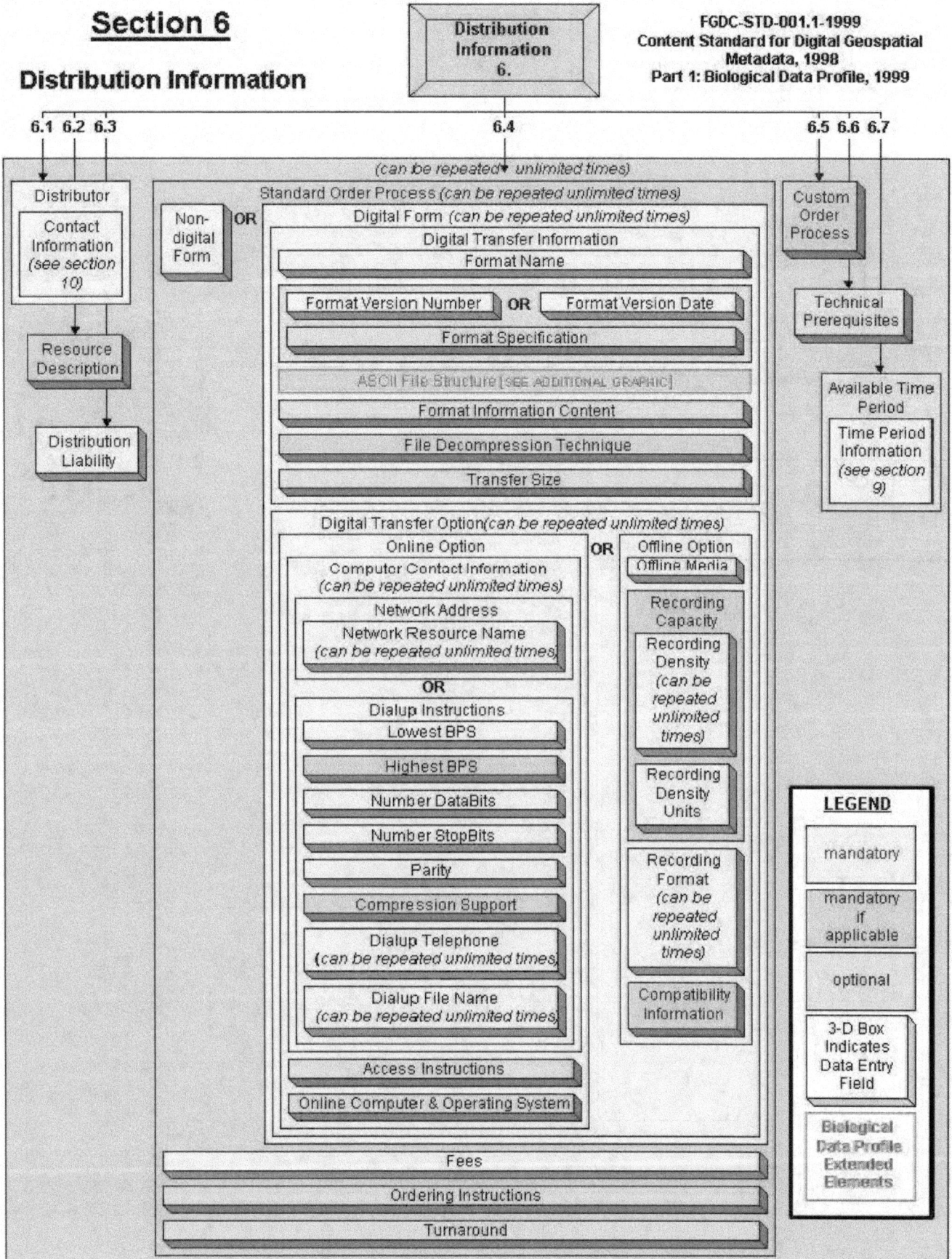

Distribution Information 6.

6.1 6.2 6.3

6.4

6.5 6.6 6.7

(can be repeated unlimited times)

Distributor

Contact Information *(see section 10)*

Resource Description

Distribution Liability

Standard Order Process *(can be repeated unlimited times)*

Non-digital Form **OR**

Digital Form *(can be repeated unlimited times)*

Digital Transfer Information

Format Name

Format Version Number **OR** Format Version Date

Format Specification

ASCII File Structure [SEE ADDITIONAL GRAPHIC]

Format Information Content

File Decompression Technique

Transfer Size

Digital Transfer Option *(can be repeated unlimited times)*

Online Option **OR** Offline Option

Computer Contact Information *(can be repeated unlimited times)*

Network Address

Network Resource Name *(can be repeated unlimited times)*

OR

Dialup Instructions

Lowest BPS

Highest BPS

Number DataBits

Number StopBits

Parity

Compression Support

Dialup Telephone *(can be repeated unlimited times)*

Dialup File Name *(can be repeated unlimited times)*

Access Instructions

Online Computer & Operating System

Offline Media

Recording Capacity

Recording Density *(can be repeated unlimited times)*

Recording Density Units

Recording Format *(can be repeated unlimited times)*

Compatibility Information

Fees

Ordering Instructions

Turnaround

Custom Order Process

Technical Prerequisites

Available Time Period

Time Period Information *(see section 9)*

LEGEND

mandatory

mandatory if applicable

optional

3-D Box Indicates Data Entry Field

Biological Data Profile Extended Elements

27

Section 7

Metadata Reference Information

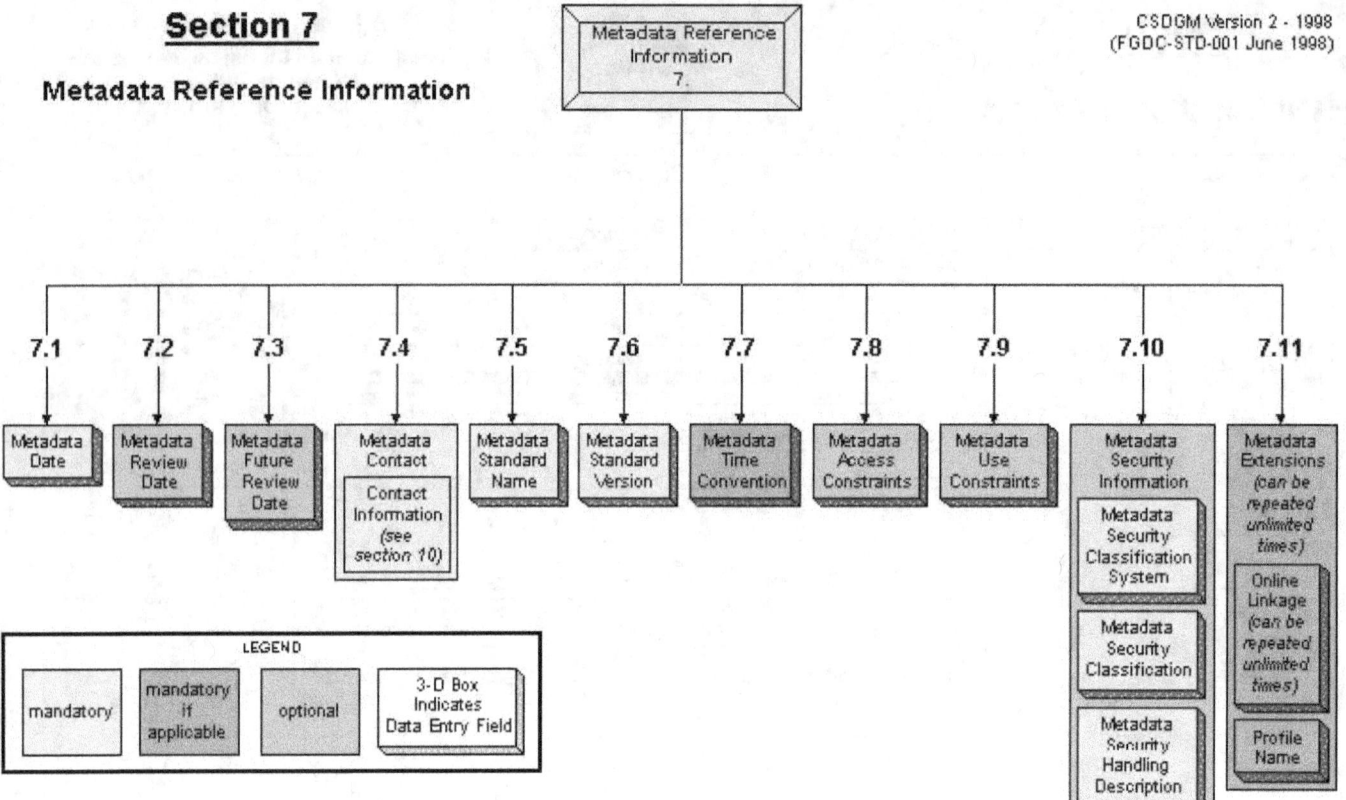

LEGEND

| mandatory | mandatory if applicable | optional | 3-D Box Indicates Data Entry Field |

Section 8

Citation Information

Citation Information

Originator
(can be repeated unlimited times)

Publication Date

Publication Time

Title

Edition

Geospatial Data Presentation Form

Series Information

Series Name

Issue Identification

Publication Information

Publication Place

Publisher

Other Citation Details

Online Linkage
(can be repeated unlimited times)

Larger Work Citation

Citation Information
(see Section 8)

Section 9

Time Period Information

Time Period Information
Single Date / Time

Calendar Date

Time of Day

OR

Geologic Age
[SEE ADDITIONAL GRAPHIC]

OR

Multiple Dates / Times
(2 or more repetitions)

Calendar Date

Time of Day

OR

Geologic Age
[SEE ADDITIONAL GRAPHIC]

OR

Range of Dates / Times

Beginning Date

Beginning Time

Ending Date

Ending Time

OR

Beginning Geologic Age

Geologic Age
[SEE ADDITIONAL GRAPHIC]

Ending Geologic Age

Geologic Age
[SEE ADDITIONAL GRAPHIC]

Section 10

Contact Information

Contact Information

Contact Person Primary

Contact Person

Contact Organization

OR

Contact Organization Primary

Contact Organization

Contact Person

Contact Position

Contact Address
(can be repeated unlimited times)

Address Type

Address
(can be repeated unlimited times)

City

State or Province

Postal Code

Country

Contact Voice Telephone
(can be repeated unlimited times)

Contact TDD/TTY Telephone
(can be repeated unlimited times)

Contact Facsimile Telephone
(can be repeated unlimited times)

Contact Electronic Mail Address
(can be repeated unlimited times)

Hours of Service

Contact Instructions

LEGEND				
mandatory	mandatory if applicable	optional	3-D Box Indicates Data Entry Field	Biological Data Profile Extended Elements

Biological Data Profile Extended Elements

Taxonomy
(from Section 1: Identification Information)

ASCII File Structure
(from Section 6: Distribution Information)

Geologic Age
(from Section 9: Time Period Information)

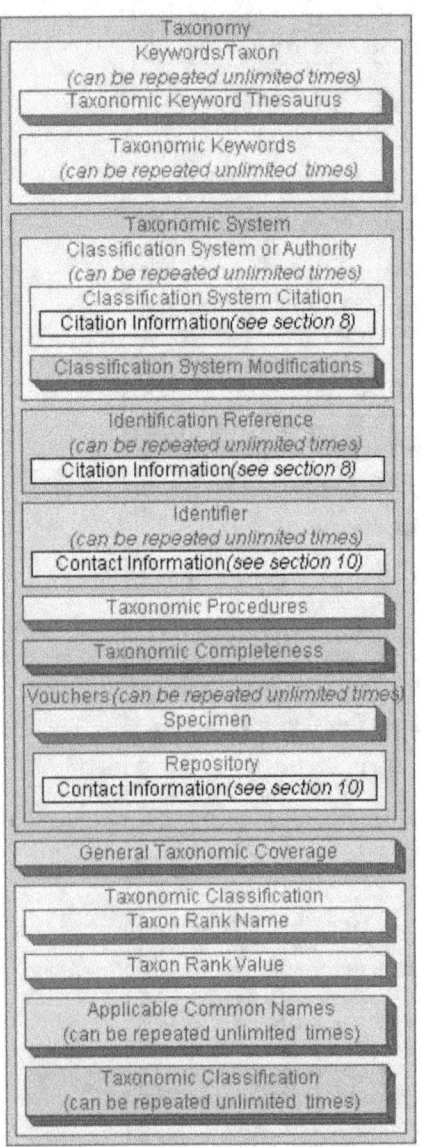

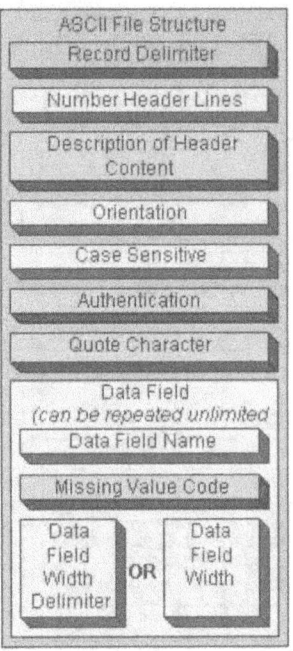

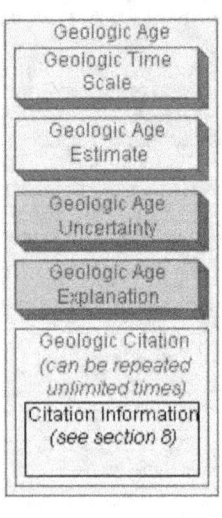

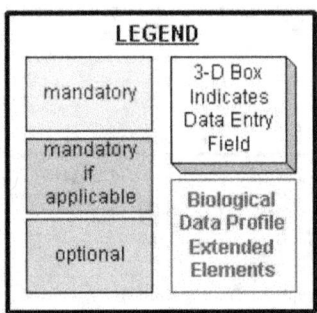